Writing
for
Fluency
and
Accuracy

Andy Boon

JN184365

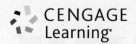

Writing for Fluency and Accuracy

Andy Boon

© 2017 Cengage Learning K.K.

ALL RIGHTS RESERVED. No part of this work covered by the copyright herein may be reproduced, transmitted, stored, or used in any form or by any means—graphic, electronic, or mechanical, including but not limited to photocopying, recording, scanning, digitizing, taping, Web distribution, information networks, or information storage and retrieval systems—without the prior written permission of the publisher.

Photo Credits:
p. 11: (l to r, t to b) © y-studio/iStock/Thinkstock, © Hideki Yoshihara/Aflo/Getty Images, © Buddhika Weerasinghe/Getty Images, © Zhang Peng/Getty Images, © Alamy/Pacific Press Service, © Bloomberg/Getty Images; p. 25: (l to r, t to b) © Tg-pint/iStock/Thinkstock, © baphotte/iStock/Thinkstock, © Bloomberg/Getty Images, © Prasit photo/Getty Images, © MIXA/Getty Images, © TAGSTOCK1/iStock/Thinkstock; p. 39: (l to r, t to b) © vindicta76/iStock/Thinkstock, © Ryhor Bruyeu/iStock/Thinkstock, © ueuaphoto/iStock/Thinkstock, © Ogovorka/iStock/Thinkstock, © Elena_Mikhailova/iStock/Thinkstock, © Lunja/iStock/Thinkstock; p. 59: (l to r, t to b) © Yiu Yu Hoi/Getty Images, © olgakr/iStock/Thinkstock, © Campus Life/Getty Images, © Andersen Ross/Getty Images, © Staras/iStock/Thinkstock, © matt_benoit/iStock/Thinkstock; p. 73: (l to r, t to b) © Brent Bossom/iStock/Thinkstock, © Koukichi Takahashi/EyeEm/Getty Images, © Poike/iStock/Thinkstock, © Bloomberg/Getty Images, © blue jean images/Getty Images, © yanyong/iStock/Thinkstock; p. 87: (l to r, t to b) © VIPDesignUSA/iStock/Thinkstock, © Mint Images/Getty Images, © Hue/amanaimagesRF/Getty Images, © Bloomberg/Getty Images, © whitetag/iStock/Thinkstock, © Campus Life/Getty Images

For permission to use material from this textbook or product, e-mail to **eltjapan@cengage.com**

ISBN: 978-4-86312-306-9

Cengage Learning K.K.
No. 2 Funato Building 5th Floor
1-11-11 Kudankita, Chiyoda-ku
Tokyo 102-0073
Japan

Tel: 03-3511-4392
Fax: 03-3511-4391

Contents

To the Student —— 4
To the Teacher —— 6

Unit 1 **Narrative Paragraphs** *Fluency* —— 11
Topic Introductions

Unit 2 **Narrative Paragraphs** *Accuracy* —— 17
Topic Memories

Unit 3 **Descriptive Paragraphs** *Fluency* —— 25
Topic Friends

Unit 4 **Descriptive Paragraphs** *Accuracy* —— 31
Topic Places

Unit 5 **Compare and Contrast Paragraphs** *Fluency* —— 39
Topic Pets

Unit 6 **Compare and Contrast Paragraphs** *Accuracy* —— 45
Topic Schools

Review 1 Review Tasks for Units 1-6 —— 52

Unit 7 **Cause and Effect Paragraphs** *Fluency* —— 59
Topic Habits

Unit 8 **Cause and Effect Paragraphs** *Accuracy* —— 65
Topic Relationships

Unit 9 **Summary Paragraphs** *Fluency* —— 73
Topic Routines

Unit 10 **Summary Paragraphs** *Accuracy* —— 79
Topic Jobs

Unit 11 **Opinion Paragraphs** *Fluency* —— 87
Topic Issues

Unit 12 **Opinion Paragraphs** *Accuracy* —— 93
Topic Smartphones

Review 2 Review Tasks for Units 7-12 —— 104

Assignments 1-6 —— 112
Chart for Recording —— 119

To the Student

Welcome to *Writing for Fluency and Accuracy*. This textbook will help you develop your English writing skills at the paragraph level. You will practice lots and lots of writing.

Writing for Fluency

In the odd units, you will do many free-writing tasks. You will write about many different topics. When we do free-writing, we write for a set period of time. We do not worry about grammar and spelling, we just write. We try to write as much as we can.

After each free-writing task, you should make a note of how many words you are able to write in the Chart for Recording at the back of the textbook.

Check your progress through the units. You should begin to write more and more as your writing fluency develops.

Writing for Accuracy

In the even units, you will be introduced to a number of different styles of writing and write a number of different paragraphs. You will plan your work, write carefully, and check and revise your drafts for mistakes.

The aim of these units is for you to work

more slowly and to pay greater attention to correcting the mistakes you make.

As you progress through these units, you should begin to write more accurately as your knowledge of English writing increases.

Keeping a Notebook

You will need to buy a B5 notebook and bring it to every class. In your notebook, you will do lots of free-writing tasks, note-taking, planning, mind-mapping/listing, and draft-writing.

Goal and Advice

Your goal is to develop your English fluency and accuracy writing skills. Here are some words of advice:
- Try to write as much as you can. We learn by doing.
- Use the Internet to help with your writing, but do not copy and paste!
- Work with your classmates. Together, you can help each other.
- Use the examples in the textbook to help guide your writing.
- Do not worry about making mistakes. Mistakes are an important part of learning a foreign language.
- Keep a well-organized notebook.
- Be proud of your work! Show it to your parents, your brothers, your sisters, and friends!

Finally, I would just like to wish you the best of luck on the journey you are about to take. I hope you study hard, have fun, and enjoy the writing course.

Andy Boon

To the Teacher

Welcome to *Writing for Fluency and Accuracy*. This textbook aims to introduce high-beginning to intermediate level students to basic writing skills at the paragraph level and to have students practice a variety of different rhetorical modes of writing.

Fluency Units

In Units 1, 3, 5, 7, and 11, students focus on writing for fluency. Students undertake a number of free-writing activities. They write for a set period of time on a given topic without paying attention to grammar and spelling. By writing extensively and freely, students can overcome mental blocks to writing in English, actually produce the language on the page, gain in confidence, and begin to write more and more as the course progresses.

A Getting Started
This section introduces students to the topic of the unit. It also provides students with language and examples they may wish to use in the free-writing tasks.

B Free-writing I
Students write a paragraph on a given topic within a negotiated period of time.

C Researching
Using their smartphones, tablets, or PCs to access the Internet, students may search for example paragraphs, useful language, and

information that other writers may include when writing.

D Free-writing II
Students write a new paragraph using the information that they found on the Internet to help them.

E Free-writing III
Students interview their classmates to get relevant information from them. They then write a new paragraph about their partner or classmates using the information that they learned at the interview stage.

F Reflecting
Students reflect on what they have learned in the unit and make a note of how many words they have written for each free-writing task.

Chart for Recording
After each free-writing task, students are instructed to write the number of words they wrote per paragraph in a chart at the back of the textbook. Here, students can track their individual progress with extensive writing. It is expected that students will begin to write longer paragraphs as they build in confidence throughout the course.

Accuracy Units

In Units 2, 4, 6, 8, and 12, students focus on writing for accuracy. Students analyze a model paragraph identifying key structural features and language. Next, they are led through a step-by-step approach to drafting their own original paragraphs. By correcting errors in a second model paragraph, students are able to raise their awareness of the common mistakes made by Japanese learners when writing. Students are then ready to check their own writing to make any necessary corrections before producing a final draft of their work.

A Getting Started
Students are able to preview language that is included within the model paragraph. Students also predict the content of the paragraph from pictures and key sentences.

B Analyzing a Paragraph
Students are introduced to a particular

rhetorical mode of writing. They read a model paragraph and identify key sentences. Comprehension questions help further develop students' awareness of key structural features and language within the paragraph.

C Mind-mapping/Listing

Students examine example mind-maps/lists based on the model paragraph of the unit. Students then create their own mind-maps/lists to help organize their thoughts before writing their own original paragraphs.

D Draft-writing

Students are led through various steps of constructing their own original paragraphs. They make a plan, compose suitable topic sentences, think about appropriate supporting sentences, consider how to conclude their paragraphs, and write their first drafts. Examples are provided to support students through the writing process.

E Completing the Draft

A second model paragraph is included for students to read. However, the paragraph contains common mistakes made by Japanese learners when writing. By working together to identify and correct the mistakes, it can raise student awareness of the types of errors they may have made in their first drafts. Before completing their final drafts, students are instructed to read through, check, and revise their own writing and that of a partner.

Summary Units

Units 9 and 10 have slightly different formats. In addition to the writing activities for fluency and accuracy, students also focus on summarizing skills. For more information on Units 9 and 10, please consult the Teacher's Manual.

Review Units

There are two review units (one that reviews Units 1–6 and the other that reviews Units 7–12). The aim is to "flip" the focus on fluency or accuracy of the previous units. For example, for the fluency units, students are given the opportunity to check and revise their free-writing paragraphs for further practice of accuracy writing. Students are also instructed to do free-writing tasks based on the topic and particular rhetorical mode of writing of each accuracy unit for further practice of fluency writing.

Assignments

There are six suggested assignments for students related to each rhetorical mode of writing included in the textbook. These offer students opportunities for further writing practice. Teachers can also set all or some of the assignments as part of the overall course assessment.

Unit 1: Narrative Paragraphs

Topic: Introductions

Fluency

A Getting Started

1 Guess

What are these pictures of? Share your ideas with your partner.

a

b

c

d

e

f

2 Connect

Match a picture to each sentence below. Write **a**–**f** in the boxes.

1. I am majoring in economics.
2. I love to read and draw manga in my free time.
3. I am a member of the dance club at university.
4. I work part-time at a convenience store.
5. I live in an apartment in Hachioji, Tokyo.
6. I have a younger brother, a younger sister, and a pet dog.

3 Discuss

Are these sentences true for you?
Share your answers with your partner.

> Sentence #1 is not true for me. I'm majoring in business management.

B Free-writing I: Interesting things about you

1 Think

Get ready to write a self-introduction paragraph. Think about interesting things about you.

2 Set the time

Decide how long you will write for and make a note of the time limit in the chart on page 119.

3 Write

Using the title and starting sentence below, write a paragraph in your notebook. Stop writing when the time is up.

> [Title]
> Interesting things about me
>
> [Starting sentence]
> There are many interesting things about me that you may not know.

4 Record

How many words did you write? Make a note of the total number in the chart on page 119.

5 Share

Pass your notebook to your partner, then share each other's paragraph. What did you learn about your partner?

> Wow! You have three older sisters. I didn't know that!

C Researching

1 Think

In order to write a self-introduction paragraph, it is useful to know what people usually write about. You can also find information about a famous person. Look at the example search terms below to get such information.

- writing self-introduction paragraph
- about {name of famous person}
-
-
-

What other search terms may help you? Add them to the list, then share your ideas with your partner.

2 Get information

Search the Internet. Use the example notes below to help you. Write down what you find in your notebook. Then, share the information with your classmates.

[Self-introduction paragraphs]

– Likes and dislikes

  http://www.manythings.org/caw/intro.html

– Where I was born

  http://www.essayforum.com/undergraduate/self-introducing-yourself-instructor-6631/

– High school attended

  http://www.famousbirthdays.com/people/lady-gaga.html

D Free-writing II: Interesting things about you

1 Think

Get ready to write a new self-introduction paragraph. Think about different information from the paragraph you wrote in Free-writing I. Use the ideas you found on the Internet to help you.

2 Set the time

Decide how long you will write for and make a note of the time limit in the chart on page 119.

3 Write

Using the title and starting sentence below, write a paragraph in your notebook. Stop writing when the time is up.

> **[Title]**
> Interesting things about me
> ....
> **[Starting sentence]**
> There are many interesting things about me that you may not know.

4 Record

How many words did you write? Make a note of the total number in the chart on page 119.

5 Share

Pass your notebook to your partner, then share each other's paragraph. What did you learn about your partner?

> Wow! Your favorite baseball team is Hanshin Tigers. Have you ever been to Koshien stadium?

E Free-writing III: About your partner

1 Think

Get ready to write an introduction paragraph about your partner. Make a list of 10 questions in your notebook to ask your partner. Use the examples to help you.

- Where do you live?
- How many brothers and sisters do you have?
- What do you like to do in your free-time?

2 Interview

Ask the questions to your partner. Take notes as you listen to the answers.

3 Set the time

Decide how long you will write for and make a note of the time limit in the chart on page 119.

4 Write

Write a paragraph in your notebook. Stop writing when the time is up.

5 Record

How many words did you write? Make a note of the total number in the chart on page 119.

6 Share

Pass your notebook to your partner, then share each other's paragraph. Is the information about you correct?

F Reflecting

▶ **Look back**

Answer the questions about Unit 1.

1. What did you learn?

2. What did you write about?

3. How many words did you write for each paragraph?

   - Free-writing I: _____ words
   - Free-writing II: _____ words
   - Free-writing III: _____ words

4. How many words per minute did you write for each paragraph?

   - Free-writing I: About _____ words per minute
   - Free-writing II: About _____ words per minute
   - Free-writing III: About _____ words per minute

Unit 2 — Narrative Paragraphs

Accuracy

Topic Memories

A Getting Started

1 Guess

What are these pictures of? Share your ideas with your partner.

2 Connect

Match a picture to each sentence below. Write a–f in the boxes.

1. However, at the end of the song, my strap came off and the guitar dropped to the floor.
2. One day, we saw an advertisement for a talent competition in the city.
3. A few years ago, my friends and I decided to form a rock band.
4. We practiced once a week in a garage.
5. We came in fourth.
6. To our surprise, we got to the next round.

3 Discuss

Using the pictures and sentences above, make a story with your partner.

B Analyzing a Narrative Paragraph

1 Understand

What is a Narrative Paragraph? Read the information below to find out.

- A Narrative Paragraph usually consists of a story and explains what happens from beginning to end.
- The starting sentence is usually the Topic Sentence. It includes the Topic and the Main Idea (what the writer will write about). Look at the example below: The circled part is the Topic and the underlined parts are the Main Idea.
  Ex There are many interesting things <u>about me</u> that you may not know.
- Supporting Sentences are placed after the Topic Sentence and they explain the story to the reader. They give information about the writer's Topic and Main Idea.
- The last sentence of the paragraph is the Concluding Sentence. It explains how the story ends and why it is important for the writer. A writer may use two or more Concluding Sentences at the end of the paragraph.

2 Skim

Quickly read the paragraph below. Find the Topic Sentence, then circle the Topic and underline the Main Idea. Use a different color pen and underline the Concluding Sentence(s).

The talent competition

One great memory of mine is getting to the final of a local talent competition with my band. A few years ago, my friends and I decided to form a rock band. I sang and played the guitar. There was also a keyboard player, a bass player, and a drummer in the band. We practiced once a week in a garage. One day, we saw an advertisement for a talent competition in the city. We decided to enter it. In the first round, we played two songs. The audience clapped and cheered loudly. We waited for the judges' results. To our surprise, we got to the next round. In the semifinals, the other bands were very good, but we did our best. Once more, we were surprised to win the semifinals and get through to the final round. On the day of the finals, the room was crowded with people. We were very nervous. We played one fast rock song. However, at the end of the song, my strap came off and the guitar dropped to the floor. It made a loud noise, but the audience enjoyed it. At the end of the competition, the judges gave their results. We came in fourth. Although we were disappointed, we enjoyed the experience very much. To quote a famous saying, "It is not the winning that matters, it is the taking part."

3 Discuss

Read the paragraph again and answer the questions in pairs/groups.

1. What is the Topic of the paragraph?

2. What is the Main Idea of the paragraph?

3. What time phrases does the writer use to tell the story?

   Ex A few years ago,

4. Read the statements about the paragraph, then circle T (True) or F (False).
   a. The writer played the drums.   T / F
   b. The writer expected to win the competition.   T / F
   c. The writer's band got to the final round.   T / F
   d. Very few people came to watch the final round.   T / F
   e. The writer was nervous in the final round.   T / F
   f. The writer's band won the competition.   T / F

5. Why is the talent competition a great memory for the writer?

6. What did the writer learn from the experience of taking part in the talent competition?

C Mind-mapping

1 Understand

Look at the mind-map below. This shows the writer's ideas before writing the paragraph you read on pages 18–19.

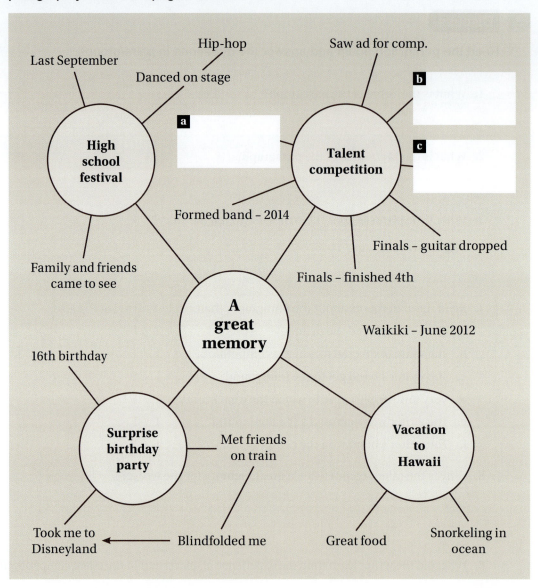

2 Discuss

Look at the mind-map again and answer the questions in pairs/groups.

1. What four great memories does the writer have?

   -
   -
   -
   -

2. Which memory did the writer choose to write about?

3. Read the paragraph on pages 18–19 again and complete boxes **a** - **c** in the mind-map.

3 Make your mind-map

Draw a circle in the middle of the page of your notebook and write "A great memory" in it. Then, make your own mind-map. Think of three or four different memories.

D Draft-writing: A great memory

1 Plan your paragraph

Look at your mind-map and choose one great memory that you would like to write about. Then, think of the title of your paragraph and make a list of the events in time order in your notebook, referring to the example below.

> ### The talent competition
> 1. Formed a band
> 2. Practiced every week
> 3. Saw an ad for talent competition
> 4. First round – played well – through to next round
> 5. Semifinals – did well – through to final
> 6. Finals – guitar dropped
> 7. Came in fourth

Remember that your list will be important when you think about your Supporting Sentences later.

2 Decide on your Topic Sentence

Think about your Topic and Main Idea, then plan your Topic Sentence. Write four different Topic Sentences in your notebook, referring to the examples below.

> 1. One great memory of mine is getting to the final of a local talent competition with my band.
> 2. I will never forget getting to the final of a local talent competition with my band.
> 3. The first time my band and I entered a local talent competition, we got to the final round.
> 4. Getting to the final of a local talent competition with my band is one of the greatest memories I have.

Show your four Topic Sentences to your partner and ask his/her opinion. Then, decide which one you like the best.

3 Think about your Supporting Sentences

Look at the list you made in Task D-1. Then, write your Supporting Sentences with time phrases in your notebook, referring to the example below.

1. Formed a band
   → A few years ago, my friends and I decided to form a rock band.
2. Practiced every week
   → After that, we practiced once a week in a garage.
3. Saw an ad for talent competition
   → One day, we saw an advertisement for a talent competition in the city.

For suitable time phrases for your Supporting Sentences, look back at your answers to Task B-3-3 on page 19, or search the Internet to find other useful examples.

4 Think about your Concluding Sentence(s)

How will you end your paragraph? Look at several ways below and write your Concluding Sentence(s) in your notebook.

- Repeat your Main Idea using different words.
- Tell the reader what you learned from the experience.
- Tell the reader why the story is important.
- Explain your feelings to the reader.
- Leave the reader with a famous saying or quotation.

5 Write your draft

Decide roughly how many words you will write and make a note of this in your notebook. Then, start writing a paragraph about your great memory. Remember to include the information below.

- A title
- A Topic Sentence
- Supporting Sentences (with time phrases)
- Concluding Sentence(s)

E Completing the Draft

1 Practice

In order to complete your draft, you need to read through it and correct any mistakes. Practice checking a draft. Read the paragraph below. Find and correct 15 mistakes. Then, share your answers with your partner.

My first vacation overseas

I will never forget the summer of 2012 because it was my first vacation overseas. My family and I go to Waikiki in Hawaii. We stayed there for three day and they had a great time. On the first day, It rained. So, we went to shopping. I buy many things. For example, new shooes, hat, and a mask for snorkeling. On the second day, I went snorkeling in the ocean. I saw much fish. On the final day, we went to a hamburg restaurant. I had a big cheeseburger. It was delicious. It was so big, I couldn't eat it all. I was enjoyed Hawaii. I hope I can go back there one day in the future.

---

2 Check your draft

Check your draft and correct any mistakes you find.

3 Check your partner's draft

Read your partner's draft and check it. If you find any mistakes, tell your partner.

4 Revise your draft

Read your draft again and think of any ways to improve it. Make any necessary revisions.

Unit 3

Descriptive Paragraphs

Topic Friends

Fluency

A Getting Started

1 Guess

What are these pictures of? Share your ideas with your partner.

a

b

c

d

e

f

2 Connect

Match a picture to each sentence below. Write **a**–**f** in the boxes.

1. She is very smart.
2. She has really short black hair.
3. She lives in the same apartment block as me.
4. She always makes me laugh when I feel sad.
5. She likes to wear baggy T-shirts.
6. She is a really good singer.

3 Discuss

Are these sentences true for your friends? Share your answers with your partner.

> Sentence #1 is true for my friend, Eri. She always gets good scores on tests.

B Free-writing I: About a friend

1 Think

Get ready to write a Descriptive Paragraph. Think about one of your closest friends.

2 Set the time

Decide how long you will write for and make a note of the time limit in the chart on page 119.

3 Write

Using the title and Topic Sentence below, write a paragraph in your notebook. Stop writing when the time is up.

> **[Title]**
> My friend
>
> ....
>
> **[Topic Sentence]**
> {name} is one of my closest friends.

4 Record

How many words did you write? Make a note of the total number in the chart on page 119.

5 Share

Pass your notebook to your partner, then share each other's paragraph. What did you learn about your partner's friend?

> Your friend is a black belt in karate. That's amazing!

C Researching

1 Think

In order to write a Descriptive Paragraph about a friend, it is useful to know what people usually write about. Look at the example search term below to get such information.

- writing descriptive paragraph friend
-
-
-

What other search terms may help you? Add them to the list, then share your ideas with your partner.

2 Get information

Search the Internet. Use the example notes below to help you. Write down what you find in your notebook. Then, share the information with your classmates.

[Descriptive Paragraphs about a friend]

– How long I have known my friend

   https://tikakm.wordpress.com/2013/06/12/descriptive-paragraph/

– My friend's age

   http://writing1propea08.blogspot.jp/2008/10/my-best-friend_5204.html

– Where my friend is from/lives now

   http://image.slidesharecdn.com/howtowriteaparagraphaboutmybestfriend-141101142609-conversion-gate01/95/how-to-write-a-paragraph-about-my-best-friend-8-638.jpg?cb=1414852123

D Free-writing II: About a friend

1 Think

Get ready to write a new Descriptive Paragraph about your friend. Think about different information from the paragraph you wrote in Free-writing I. Use the ideas you found on the Internet to help you.

2 Set the time

Decide how long you will write for and make a note of the time limit in the chart on page 119.

3 Write

Using the title and Topic Sentence below, write a paragraph in your notebook. Stop writing when the time is up.

> **[Title]**
> My friend
> ....
> **[Topic Sentence]**
> {name} is one of my closest friends.

4 Record

How many words did you write? Make a note of the total number in the chart on page 119.

5 Share

Pass your notebook to your partner, then share each other's paragraph. What did you learn about your partner's friend?

> Your friend was born in the States, but moved to Japan when he was three years old. That's very interesting!

E Free-writing III: About your partner's friend

1 Think

Get ready to write a Descriptive Paragraph about your partner's friend. Make a list of 10 questions in your notebook to ask your partner. Use the examples to help you.

- What's your friend's name?
- What does he/she look like?
- What is he/she like?

2 Interview

Ask the questions to your partner. Take notes as you listen to the answers.

3 Set the time

Decide how long you will write for and make a note of the time limit in the chart on page 119.

4 Write

Write a paragraph in your notebook. Stop writing when the time is up.

5 Record

How many words did you write? Make a note of the total number in the chart on page 119.

6 Share

Pass your notebook to your partner, then share each other's paragraph. Is the information about your friend correct?

F Reflecting

▶ Look back

Answer the questions about Unit 3.

1. What did you learn?

2. What did you write about?

3. How many words did you write for each paragraph?
   - Free-writing I: _____ words
   - Free-writing II: _____ words
   - Free-writing III: _____ words

4. How many words per minute did you write for each paragraph?
   - Free-writing I: About _____ words per minute
   - Free-writing II: About _____ words per minute
   - Free-writing III: About _____ words per minute

Unit 4: Descriptive Paragraphs

Topic: Places

Accuracy

A Getting Started

1 Guess

What are these pictures of? Share your ideas with your partner.

2 Connect

Match a picture to each sentence below. Write a–f in the boxes.

1. The park has lots of green grass and many tall trees.
2. I like to walk around it.
3. The park has a long, circular path.
4. Next to the pond, there is a little store that sells food and drink.
5. I live in the city with lots of gray, high-rise buildings.
6. The pond is full of colorful fish.

3 Discuss

What is described in the pictures and sentences above? What extra information may the writer give? Share your answers with your partner.

B Analyzing a Descriptive Paragraph

1 Understand

What is a Descriptive Paragraph? Read the information below to find out.

- A Descriptive Paragraph gives the reader information about a person, a place, or an item. This description helps the reader to imagine. It helps the reader to see, taste, touch, smell, and/or hear what you are describing.
- The starting sentence is usually the Topic Sentence. It includes the Topic and the Main Idea (what the writer will write about).
- Supporting Sentences are placed after the Topic Sentence and they describe important details to the reader.
- Extra Information Sentences give more information about each important detail.
- The last sentence of the paragraph is the Concluding Sentence. It reminds the reader of the Topic and summarizes the ideas written about in the paragraph. A writer may use two or more Concluding Sentences at the end of the paragraph.

2 Skim

Quickly read the paragraph below. Find the Topic Sentence, then circle the Topic and underline the Main Idea. Use a different color pen and underline the Concluding Sentence(s).

My favorite place

I live in the city with lots of gray, high-rise buildings. Therefore, the park across from my apartment is my favorite place to go in my free time. It has lots of green grass and many tall trees. When I visit the park, I soon forget about life in the busy city. The park also has a long, circular path. I like to walk around it. It is good exercise and I can hear the relaxing sound of birds and insects. It feels like being in the countryside. In the center of the park is a large pond. The pond is full of colorful fish. I sometimes sit and watch them swim around. It is so peaceful. Next to the pond, there is a little store that sells food and drink. In the summer, I often buy green tea ice cream cones. They are very delicious to eat on a hot day. All in all, the park is a great place for me to escape the city, to relax, and to enjoy some peace and quiet.

3 Discuss

Read the paragraph again and answer the questions in pairs/groups.

1. What is the Topic of the paragraph?

2. What is the Main Idea of the paragraph?

3. What four important details about the park does the writer include in her description?

   -
   -
   -
   -

4. Find 10 adjectives that the writer uses in her description. Why do you think the writer uses these adjectives?

5. What extra information do we learn about the writer and the park?

   Ex The writer goes to the park to escape the city.

C Mind-mapping

1 Understand

Look at the mind-map below. This shows the writer's ideas before writing the paragraph you read on page 32.

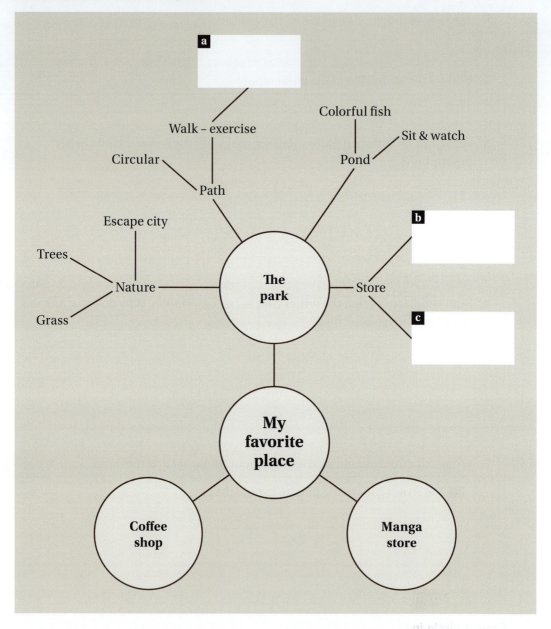

2 Discuss

Look at the mind-map again and answer the questions in pairs/groups.

1. Read the paragraph on page 32 again and complete boxes **a** - **c** in the mind-map.
2. If you were the writer, what ideas would you add to the circle of "Coffee shop" or "Manga store"? Choose one of them and make a mind-map below.

3 Make your mind-map

Draw a circle in the middle of the page of your notebook and write "My favorite place" in it. Then, make your own mind-map. Think of three or four different places.

D Draft-writing: Your favorite place

1 Plan your paragraph

Look at your mind-map and choose one place that you would like to write about. Then, think of the title of your paragraph and make a plan of how best to describe your place in your notebook, referring to the example below.

> **My favorite place**
> 1. Topic Sentence – why park is favorite place
> 2. Nature vs. City – grass and trees
> 3. Circular path
> 4. Pond in center
> 5. Store next to pond
> 6. Concluding Sentence(s) – relaxing place

Remember that your plan will be important when you think about your Supporting Sentences later.

2 Decide on your Topic Sentence

Think about your Topic and Main Idea, then plan your Topic Sentence. Write four different Topic Sentences in your notebook, referring to the examples below.

> 1. The park across from my apartment is my favorite place to go in my free time.
> 2. My favorite place is the park across from my apartment.
> 3. The park across from my apartment is a wonderful place to spend time.
> 4. Across from my apartment is a beautiful, green park.

Show your four Topic Sentences to your partner and ask his/her opinion. Then, decide which one you like the best.

3 Think about your Supporting Sentences

Look at the plan you made in Task D-1. Then, write your Supporting Sentences in your notebook. For example sentences, look back at your answers to Task B-3-3 on page 33.

Unit 4 Descriptive Paragraphs **Accuracy**

4 Think about your Extra Information Sentences

Write your Extra Information Sentences in your notebook, referring to the example below.

> **[Detail]**
> Circular path
>
> **[Extra information]**
> – I walk around the path.
> – I can exercise.
> – I can hear beautiful sounds of insects and birds.
> – It feels like I am in the countryside.

5 Think about your Concluding Sentence(s)

How will you end your paragraph? Look at several ways below and write your Concluding Sentence(s) in your notebook.

> - Summarize your main details using different words.
> - Repeat why it is your favorite place using different words.
> - Explain your feelings about the place to the reader.
> - Leave the reader with a final comment about the place.
> - Leave the reader with a final suggestion.

6 Write your draft

Decide roughly how many words you will write and make a note of this in your notebook. Then, start writing a paragraph about your favorite place. Remember to include the information below.

> - A title
> - A Topic Sentence
> - Supporting Sentences
> - Extra Information Sentences
> - Concluding Sentence(s)

E Completing the Draft

1 Practice

In order to complete your draft, you need to read through it and correct any mistakes. Practice checking a draft. Read the paragraph below. Find and correct 15 mistakes. Then, share your answers with your partner.

My favorite place

My favorite place is the local coffee shop next to my university in the Gotanda. The coffee shop is called "Café Mama." It's very small and looks quite old.

There are only four wooden table inside and old leather sofa. So I often have to waiting for a seat. But, when I open the door, there is always a wonderful smell of freshly roasted coffee in the air. It is very welcoming and wakes me up in the mornings. My classes start at nine. The owner is a friendly, old woman. She always say good morning to me and asks me how I am doing. She knows my name. Because I am a regular customer. I always order a tall caffè ratte from her. He serves it in a red and white mug. It is very hot and tastes delicious. As well as sell coffee, the shop sells homemade food. Once a week, I order a slice of blueberry cheesecake. It is very sweet. When I eat the cheesecake, it melts on my tongue. I really love it. If you are ever in Gotanda, why not "Café Mama" for a coffee and a slice of cake?

---

2 Check your draft

Check your draft and correct any mistakes you find.

3 Check your partner's draft

Read your partner's draft and check it. If you find any mistakes, tell your partner.

4 Revise your draft

Read your draft again and think of any ways to improve it. Make any necessary revisions.

Unit 5

Compare and Contrast Paragraphs

Topic: **Pets**

A Getting Started

1 Guess

What are these pictures of? Share your ideas with your partner.

2 Connect

Match a picture to each sentence below. Write **a**–**f** in the boxes.

1. Unlike cats, dogs need walking.
2. On the other hand, cats can clean themselves.
3. Cats can climb trees whereas dogs cannot.
4. Dogs are more loyal than cats.
5. However, dogs can protect their owners.
6. Moreover, stroking dogs helps to lower stress.

3 Discuss

Which do you like better, cats or dogs?
Share your answers with your partner.

> I like cats because they are less expensive to keep than dogs.

B Free-writing I: Two popular pets

1 Think

Get ready to write a Contrast Paragraph. Think about two pets that are very different.

2 Set the time

Decide how long you will write for and make a note of the time limit in the chart on page 119.

3 Write

Using the title and Topic Sentence below, write a paragraph in your notebook. Stop writing when the time is up.

> **[Title]**
> Two popular pets
>
> **[Topic Sentence]**
> Although {Pet A} and {Pet B} are both popular pets, {Pet A/B} are better than {Pet A/B}.

4 Record

How many words did you write? Make a note of the total number in the chart on page 119.

5 Share

Pass your notebook to your partner, then share each other's paragraph. What did you learn about your partner's ideas?

> You have tropical fish. You think that having fish is more relaxing than having a cat, right?

Unit 5　Compare and Contrast Paragraphs　Fluency

C　Researching

1　Think

In order to write a Contrast Paragraph about two different pets, it is useful to know what people usually write about, or to find information about how to write Contrast Paragraphs. Look at the example search term below to get such information.

- Dogs vs. Cats as pets
-
-
-

What other search terms may help you? Add them to the list, then share your ideas with your partner.

2　Get information

Search the Internet. Use the example notes below to help you. Write down what you find in your notebook. Then, share the information with your classmates.

[Contrast Paragraphs about two pets]

– Differences between cats and dogs

　　　http://healthypets.mercola.com/sites/healthypets/archive/2011/01/04/

　　　differences-between-pet-cats-and-pet-dogs.aspx

- dogs are easy to train

– Language for Contrast Paragraphs

　　　http://www2.actden.com/writ_den/tips/paragrap/compare.htm

- However,
- On the other hand,

D Free-writing II: Two popular pets

1 Think

Get ready to write a new Contrast Paragraph about the two pets. Think about different information from the paragraph you wrote in Free-writing I. Use the ideas you found on the Internet to help you.

2 Set the time

Decide how long you will write for and make a note of the time limit in the chart on page 119.

3 Write

Using the title and Topic Sentence below, write a paragraph in your notebook. Stop writing when the time is up.

> **[Title]**
> Two popular pets
>
> **[Topic Sentence]**
> Although {Pet A} and {Pet B} are both popular pets, {Pet A/B} are better than {Pet A/B}.

4 Record

How many words did you write? Make a note of the total number in the chart on page 119.

5 Share

Pass your notebook to your partner, then share each other's paragraph. What did you learn about your partner's ideas?

> You prefer dogs to cats because your dog welcomes you when you get home from school. However, your cat ignores you, right?

E Free-writing III: You and your partner

1 Think

Get ready to write a Contrast Paragraph about you and your partner. Make a list of 10 questions in your notebook to ask your partner to find differences between you. Use the examples to help you.

> – Do you have any pets?
>
> – Which do you like better, cats or dogs?
>
> – What do you do to lower stress?

2 Interview

Ask the questions to your partner. Take notes as you listen to the answers.

3 Set the time

Decide how long you will write for and make a note of the time limit in the chart on page 119.

4 Write

Write a paragraph in your notebook. Stop writing when the time is up.

5 Record

How many words did you write? Make a note of the total number in the chart on page 119.

6 Share

Pass your notebook to your partner, then share each other's paragraph. What differences are there between you and your partner?

F Reflecting

▶ **Look back**

Answer the questions about Unit 5.

1. What did you learn?

2. What did you write about?

3. How many words did you write for each paragraph?
   - Free-writing I: _____ words
   - Free-writing II: _____ words
   - Free-writing III: _____ words

4. How many words per minute did you write for each paragraph?
   - Free-writing I: About _____ words per minute
   - Free-writing II: About _____ words per minute
   - Free-writing III: About _____ words per minute

Unit 6

Compare and Contrast Paragraphs

Accuracy

Topic: **Schools**

A Getting Started

1 Guess

What are these pictures of? Share your ideas with your partner.

2 Connect

Match a picture to each sentence below. Write **a**–**f** in the boxes.

1. Therefore, I have volleyball practice on Saturdays and Sundays.
2. When I started university, I decided to join the volleyball team again.
3. At high school, I studied English four times a week.
4. We always have lunch together in the cafeteria.
5. We meet during the vacation time and go to karaoke.
6. I have to stay up late every night doing my homework.

3 Discuss

What is compared in the pictures and sentences above? What similarities may the writer describe? Share your answers with your partner.

B Analyzing a Compare and Contrast Paragraph

1 Understand

What is a Compare and Contrast Paragraph? Read the information below to find out.

- A Compare and Contrast Paragraph either discusses how two things are alike, different, or both alike and different. The writer gives examples of the similarities and/or differences between a Topic that includes two subjects
- The starting sentence is usually the Topic Sentence. It includes the Topic nd the Main Idea (whether the writer will compare and/or contrast the two subjects).
- Supporting Sentences are placed after the Topic Sentence and they describe the main points of similarity and/or difference between the two subjects within the Topic.
- Extra Information Sentences give more information about each main point.
- The last sentence of the paragraph is the Concluding Sentence. It reminds the reader of the Topic (Subjects A and B) and whether the writer feels they are similar or different. A writer may use two or more Concluding Sentences at the end of the paragraph.

2 Skim

Quickly read the paragraph below. Find the Topic Sentence, then circle the Topic (Subjects A and B) and underline the Main Idea. Use a different color pen and underline the Concluding Sentence(s).

High school and university life

Starting a new school is a big change for me. However, there are many similarities between my old life at high school and my current life at university. For example, at high school, I studied English four times a week and really enjoyed it. Similarly, at university, I have a listening, reading, speaking, and writing class. They are all really fun. Also, I used to belong to the volleyball team at high school. The team practiced hard and I often had to go to school on weekends to play. When I started university, I decided to join the volleyball team again. Therefore, I have volleyball practice on Saturdays and Sundays and am as busy as I was at high school. Another similarity is the amount of homework I have. At high school, I always had a lot of homework. At university, it is just the same. I have to stay up late every night doing it. Finally, at both places, I have made great friends. I am still in touch with my old high school friends. We meet during the vacation time and go to karaoke. At university, I have met some really nice people in my classes. We always have lunch together in the cafeteria. In a way, although university is new and exciting for me, my life is pretty much the same as when I was at high school.

3 Discuss

Read the paragraph again and answer the questions in pairs/groups.

1. What is the Topic (Subjects A and B) of the paragraph?

2. What is the Main Idea of the paragraph?

3. What four points of similarity does the writer include in her paragraph?
   -
   -
   -
   -

4. Find five words/phrases that the writer uses to show comparison.

   Ex again

5. How does the writer feel about university in her Concluding Sentence?

C Listing

1 Understand

Look at the list below. This shows the writer's ideas before writing the paragraph you read on pages 46–47. Where the circles overlap, there are points of comparison between the Topic (Subjects A and B). Where the circles do not overlap, there are points of contrast between the two subjects.

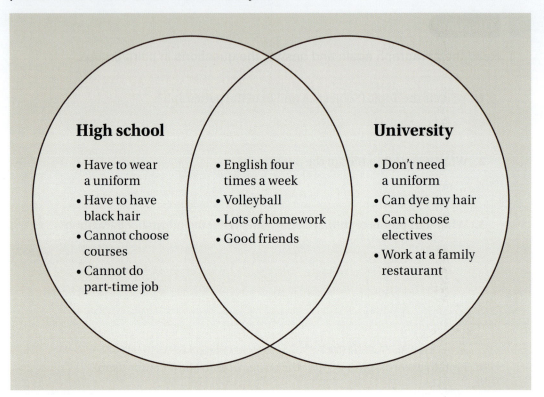

2 Discuss

Look at the list above and read the paragraph on pages 46–47 again. You can see that the writer chose to write about the similarities between high school and university. Now, imagine the writer chose to write about the differences. How would the paragraph be different? Discuss in pairs/groups.

3 Make your list

Draw two big, overlapping circles in your notebook and write your two subjects in each circle. Then, make your own list about the Topic (Subjects A and B).

D Draft-writing: Two subjects

1 Plan your paragraph

Look at your list and decide whether you will compare and/or contrast the two subjects within the Topic. Then, think of the title of your paragraph and make a plan of how best to order your main points in your notebook, referring to the example below.

High school and university life

1. Topic Sentence – many similarities
2. Same number of English classes
3. Joined volleyball team
4. Same amount of homework
5. Made good friends
6. Concluding Sentence(s) – life pretty much the same

Remember that your plan will be important when you think about your Supporting Sentences later.

2 Decide on your Topic Sentence

Think about your Topic (Subjects A and B) and Main Idea, then plan your Topic Sentence. Write four different Topic Sentences in your notebook, referring to the examples below.

1. There are many similarities between my old high school life and my current life at university.
2. I have found that being at high school and being at university are not that much different.
3. My life now at university and my life last year at high school are very different.
4. Several similarities and differences exist between my life at high school and my life at university.

Show your four Topic Sentences to your partner and ask his/her opinion. Then, decide which one you like the best.

3 Think about your Supporting Sentences

Look at the plan you made in Task D-1. Then, write your Supporting Sentences with words/phrases to show comparison and/or contrast in your notebook, referring to the example below.

1. Same number of English classes
   → Similarly, at university, I have a listening, reading, speaking, and writing class.
2. Joined volleyball team
   → When I started university, I decided to join the volleyball team again.
3. Same amount of homework
   → Another similarity is the amount of homework.
4. Made good friends
   → Finally, at both places, I have made great friends.

For suitable words/phrases, look back at your answers to Task B-3-4 on page 47, or search the Internet to find other useful examples.

4 Think about your Concluding Sentence(s)

How will you end your paragraph? Look at several ways below and write your Concluding Sentence(s) in your notebook.

- Summarize your main points using different words.
- Repeat your Topic Sentence using different words.
- Explain your final feelings to the reader.

5 Write your draft

Decide roughly how many words you will write and make a note of this in your notebook. Then, start writing a paragraph about your Topic (Subjects A and B). Remember to include the following information.

- A title
- A Topic Sentence
- Supporting Sentences
- Words/Phrases to show comparison and/or contrast
- Extra Information Sentences
- Concluding Sentence(s)

Unit 6 Compare and Contrast Paragraphs Accuracy

E Completing the Draft

1 Practice

In order to complete your draft, you need to read through it and correct any mistakes. Practice checking a draft. Read the paragraph below. Find and correct 15 mistakes. Then, share your answers with your partner.

High school and university life

Starting university has been a big change for me. Because there are many difference from my life at high school. The first big difference is that I now live in dormitory. At high school, I lived at home and my parents use to do all of the cook and cleaning. However now I have to do anything for myself. Another difference is that I no longer have to wear an uniform. At high school, it was easy for me to get ready in the morning. However, I now have to what to wear each day. This takes me many time and sometimes I am late for class. A final change is that as a university student, I can do arbeito, whereas at high school, this was not allowed. I just start working three times a week at a famiry restaurant near the campus. This is fun, but it means I am really busy these days. Therefore, although university is excited for me, I have to be very care to mange my time and my schoolwork.

---

2 Check your draft

Check your draft and correct any mistakes you find.

3 Check your partner's draft

Read your partner's draft and check it. If you find any mistakes, tell your partner.

4 Revise your draft

Read your draft again and think of any ways to improve it. Make any necessary revisions.

Review 1

Review Tasks for Units 1–6

Unit 1 Narrative Paragraphs — Accuracy

1 Look back

You practiced writing for fluency in Unit 1. What did you study? What did you write about? Share your answers with your partner.

2 Review common mistakes

Look at your answers for Task E-1 in Unit 2 (page 24), Unit 4 (page 38), and Unit 6 (page 51) to review the common mistakes made when writing.

3 Check your drafts

Now, you will focus on accuracy using your drafts for Free-writing I, II, and III. Check your drafts in your notebook and correct any mistakes you find.

4 Check your partner's drafts

Read your partner's drafts and check them. If you find any mistakes, tell your partner.

5 Revise for accuracy

Read your drafts again and think of any ways to improve them. Make any necessary revisions.

Unit 2 Narrative Paragraphs

Fluency

1 Look back

You practiced writing for accuracy in Unit 2. What did you study? What did you write about? Share your answers with your partner.

2 Think

In Unit 2, you wrote a Narrative Paragraph about a great memory. Now, get ready to write a new Narrative Paragraph. Think about another great memory you have had in your life.

3 Set the time

Now, you will practice writing for fluency. Decide how long you will write for and make a note of the time limit in the chart on page 119.

4 Write for fluency

Write a paragraph in your notebook. Stop writing when the time is up.

5 Record

How many words did you write? Make a note of the total number in the chart on page 119.

6 Share

Pass your notebook to your partner, then share each other's paragraph. What did you learn about your partner?

Unit 3 Descriptive Paragraphs　　　Accuracy

1 Look back

You practiced writing for fluency in Unit 3. What did you study? What did you write about? Share your answers with your partner.

2 Review common mistakes

Look at your answers for Task E-1 in Unit 2 (page 24), Unit 4 (page 38), and Unit 6 (page 51) to review the common mistakes made when writing.

3 Check your drafts

Now, you will focus on accuracy using your drafts for Free-writing I, II, and III. Check your drafts in your notebook and correct any mistakes you find.

4 Check your partner's drafts

Read your partner's drafts and check them. If you find any mistakes, tell your partner.

5 Revise for accuracy

Read your drafts again and think of any ways to improve them. Make any necessary revisions.

Review 1
Review Tasks for Units 1–6

Unit 4 Descriptive Paragraphs **Fluency**

1 Look back

You practiced writing for accuracy in Unit 4. What did you study? What did you write about? Share your answers with your partner.

2 Think

In Unit 4, you wrote a Descriptive Paragraph about your favorite place. Now, get ready to write a new Descriptive Paragraph. Think about another place you really like.

3 Set the time

Now, you will practice writing for fluency. Decide how long you will write for and make a note of the time limit in the chart on page 119.

4 Write for fluency

Write a paragraph in your notebook. Stop writing when the time is up.

5 Record

How many words did you write? Make a note of the total number in the chart on page 119.

6 Share

Pass your notebook to your partner, then share each other's paragraph. What did you learn about your partner?

Unit 5 Compare and Contrast Paragraphs — Accuracy

1 Look back

You practiced writing for fluency in Unit 5. What did you study? What did you write about? Share your answers with your partner.

2 Review common mistakes

Look at your answers for Task E-1 in Unit 2 (page 24), Unit 4 (page 38), and Unit 6 (page 51) to review the common mistakes made when writing.

3 Check your drafts

Now, you will focus on accuracy using your drafts for Free-writing I, II, and III. Check your drafts in your notebook and correct any mistakes you find.

4 Check your partner's drafts

Read your partner's drafts and check them. If you find any mistakes, tell your partner.

5 Revise for accuracy

Read your drafts again and think of any ways to improve them. Make any necessary revisions.

Review 1
Review Tasks for Units 1–6

Unit 6 Compare and Contrast Paragraphs — Fluency

1 Look back

You practiced writing for accuracy in Unit 6. What did you study? What did you write about? Share your answers with your partner.

2 Think

In Unit 6, you wrote a Compare and/or Contrast Paragraph about a Topic (Subjects A and B). Now, get ready to write a new Compare and/or Contrast Paragraph. Think about another Topic (Subjects A and B) to compare and/or contrast.

3 Set the time

Now, you will practice writing for fluency. Decide how long you will write for and make a note of the time limit in the chart on page 119.

4 Write for fluency

Write a paragraph in your notebook. Stop writing when the time is up.

5 Record

How many words did you write? Make a note of the total number in the chart on page 119.

6 Share

Pass your notebook to your partner, then share each other's paragraph. What did you learn about your partner's ideas?

Unit 7
Cause and Effect Paragraphs

Fluency

Topic Habits

A Getting Started

1 Guess

What are these pictures of? Share your ideas with your partner.

2 Connect

Match a picture to each sentence below. Write **a**–**f** in the boxes.

1. As a result, I get lots of exercise every day.
2. Therefore, I sometimes get bad scores in my assignments.
3. This is because I eat too much junk food.
4. Another reason is that I eat a lot of vegetables.
5. I text my friends at night, so I do not get enough sleep.
6. I am always busy because I have too much homework to do.

3 Discuss

Are these sentences about causes only, effects only, or both causes and effects?

> I think sentence #1 is an effect. The cause might be cycling to school every day. What do you think?

B Free-writing I: Your habits

1 Think

Get ready to write a Cause and/or Effect Paragraph. Think about your habits.

2 Set the time

Decide how long you will write for and make a note of the time limit in the chart on page 119.

3 Write

Think of the title and Topic Sentence, then write a paragraph in your notebook. Use the example to help you. Stop writing when the time is up.

> **[Title]**
> My study habits
>
> **[Topic Sentence]**
> As a student, I study really hard and this has a number of positive effects for me.

4 Record

How many words did you write? Make a note of the total number in the chart on page 119.

5 Share

Pass your notebook to your partner, then share each other's paragraph. What did you learn about your partner?

> You always forget to do your homework because you have two part-time jobs. Wow!

C Researching

1 Think

In order to write a Cause and/or Effect Paragraph about your habits, it is useful to know what people usually write about. Look at the example search term below to get such information.

- cause and effect example sentences
-
-
-

What other search terms may help you? Add them to the list, then share your ideas with your partner.

2 Get information

Search the Internet. Use the example notes below to help you. Write down what you find in your notebook. Then, share the information with your classmates.

[Cause and Effect Paragraphs]

– Example sentences

  http://examples.yourdictionary.com/cause-and-effect-examples.html

  - X happened and as a result, Y happened.
  - Since X happened, Y happened.

– Linking words

  http://web2.uvcs.uvic.ca/elc/studyzone/570/pulp/hemp5.htm

  - Consequently, X
  - X happened due to Y

D Free-writing II: Your habits

1 Think

Get ready to write a new Cause and/or Effect Paragraph about your habits. Think about different information from the paragraph you wrote in Free-writing I. Use the ideas you found on the Internet to help you.

2 Set the time

Decide how long you will write for and make a note of the time limit in the chart on page 119.

3 Write

Think of the title and Topic Sentence, then write a paragraph in your notebook. Stop writing when the time is up.

4 Record

How many words did you write? Make a note of the total number in the chart on page 119.

5 Share

Pass your notebook to your partner, then share each other's paragraph. What did you learn about your partner?

> You like to exercise, so you use the stairs at university instead of the elevators. That's a great idea.

E Free-writing III: Your classmates' habits

1 Think

Get ready to write a Cause and/or Effect Paragraph about your classmates' habits. Make a list of 10 questions in your notebook to ask your classmates. Use the examples to help you.

- What are your good habits?
- What are your bad habits?
- What are the causes and effects?

2 Interview

Ask the questions to your classmates. Take notes as you listen to the answers.

3 Set the time

Decide how long you will write for and make a note of the time limit in the chart on page 119.

4 Write

Write a paragraph in your notebook. Stop writing when the time is up.

5 Record

How many words did you write? Make a note of the total number in the chart on page 119.

6 Share

Pass your notebook to your partner, then share each other's paragraph. What did you find out about your classmates?

F Reflecting

▶ Look back

Answer the questions about Unit 7.

1. What did you learn?

2. What did you write about?

3. How many words did you write for each paragraph?
   - Free-writing I: _____ words
   - Free-writing II: _____ words
   - Free-writing III: _____ words

4. How many words per minute did you write for each paragraph?
   - Free-writing I: About _____ words per minute
   - Free-writing II: About _____ words per minute
   - Free-writing III: About _____ words per minute

Unit 8: Cause and Effect Paragraphs

Accuracy

Topic: Relationships

A Getting Started

1 Guess

What are these pictures of? Share your ideas with your partner.

2 Connect

Match a picture to each sentence below. Write **a**–**f** in the boxes.

1. We may work together doing the same part-time job.
2. We must find time in our busy schedules to meet our friends.
3. These people are friendly, funny, and interesting.
4. A good friendship develops from our efforts to help each other.
5. For example, we may be in the same club at school.
6. We have something we can easily talk about together.

3 Discuss

What is described in the pictures and sentences above? What causes may the writer explain? Share your answers with your partner.

B Analyzing a Cause and Effect Paragraph

1 Understand

What is a Cause and Effect Paragraph? Read the information below to find out.

- A Cause and Effect Paragraph discusses why something happens and/or what are its results. The writer gives examples to help the reader understand each cause and/or effect.
- The starting sentence is usually the Topic Sentence. It includes the Topic and the Main Idea (whether the writer will write about causes, effects, or causes and effects).
- Supporting Sentences are placed after the Topic Sentence and they describe each cause and/or effect.
- Extra Information Sentences give more information about each main point.
- The last sentence of the paragraph is the Concluding Sentence. It reminds the reader of the Topic and summarizes the ideas written about in the paragraph. A writer may use two or more Concluding Sentences at the end of the paragraph.

2 Skim

Quickly read the paragraph below. Find the Topic Sentence, then circle the Topic and underline the Main Idea. Use a different color pen and underline the Concluding Sentence(s).

How good friendship happens

    Most of us make good friends with other people throughout our lives. There are a number of important factors that can help friendships to develop. The first factor in a good friendship is that we often make friends with people who are in a similar situation to us. For example, we may be in the same club at school, in the same class, or we may work together doing the same part-time job. This means we have something important in common and something we can easily talk about together. The second factor in making friends is chemistry. There are people that we immediately feel comfortable to be around. These people are friendly, funny, and interesting. They are easy to talk to, easy to get along with, and easy to like. Due to this, we feel interested in getting to know them further. The final factor in developing a friendship is putting in time and effort. We must find time in our busy schedules to meet our friends. This is because it is important to go out and share experiences together. Also, a good friendship develops from our efforts to listen to, understand, and help each other when we have problems. Therefore, whoever your good friends are today, there were many factors involved in developing these friendships.

3 Discuss

Read the paragraph again and answer the questions in pairs/groups.

1. What is the Topic of the paragraph?

2. What is the Main Idea of the paragraph?

3. What three causes of good friendship does the writer include in his/her paragraph?
   -
   -
   -

4. What extra information does the writer provide about each cause?
   -
   -
   -

5. Find five words/phrases that the writer uses to show causes.

   Ex The first factor…

6. How does the writer remind the reader of his/her Topic Sentence in the Concludng Sentence?

C Listing

1 Understand

Look at the list below. This shows the writer's ideas before writing the paragraph you read on pages 66–67.

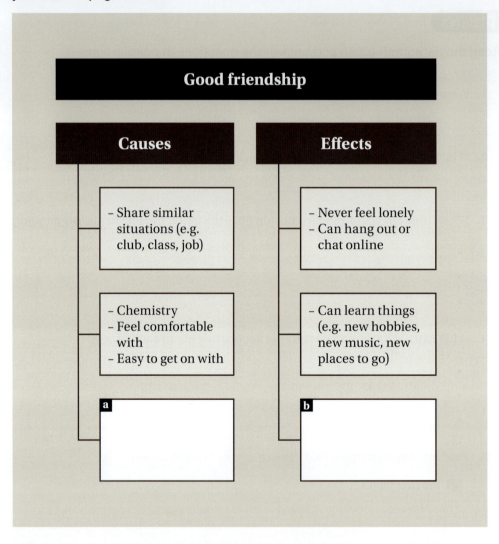

2 Discuss

Read the paragraph on pages 66–67 again, then complete box **a** in the list. Think about other effects of good friendship and complete box **b**.

3 Prepare

Think of possible Topics for a Cause and Effect Paragraph about relationships between people. Then, write them in your notebook, referring to the examples below.

- a good/bad teacher
- fights between friends
- having a boyfriend/girlfriend
- good/bad manners
- bullying
- being shy

4 Make your list

Choose one Topic and make your own list in your notebook.

D Draft-writing: Relationships between people

1 Plan your paragraph

Look at your list and decide whether you will write about the causes and/or effects of your Topic. Then, think of the title of your paragraph and make a plan of how best to order your main points in your notebook, referring to the example below.

> **Having a boyfriend/girlfriend at university**
>
> 1. Topic Sentence – many positive effects
> 2. Can share time together – dates
> 3. Can talk deeply about many things
> 4. Can get help with my problems
> 5. Concluding Sentence(s) – beneficial to have boyfriend/girlfriend

Remember that your plan will be important when you think about your Supporting Sentences later.

2 Decide on your Topic Sentence

Think about your Topic and Main Idea, then plan your Topic Sentence. Write four different Topic Sentences in your notebook, referring to the examples below.

> 1. There are many positive effects to having a boyfriend/girlfriend at university.
> 2. The main positive effect to having a boyfriend/girlfriend at university is having somebody to go on dates with, talk together, and help each other with problems.
> 3. Having a boyfriend/girlfriend at university may have three important effects on us.
> 4. Having a boyfriend/girlfriend at university may affect us in several different ways.

Show your four Topic Sentences to your partner and ask his/her opinion. Then, decide which one you like the best.

Unit 8 Cause and Effect Paragraphs **Accuracy**

3. Think about your Supporting Sentences

Look at the plan you made in Task D-1. Then, write your Supporting Sentences with words/phrases to show causes and/or effects in your notebook. Refer to the examples below for effect sentences.

> 1. Can share time together – dates
>   → Firstly, if we are in a relationship, we have somebody to share our free time with.
> 2. Can talk deeply about many things
>   → Another positive effect is having somebody to talk deeply with about many different things.
> 3. Can get help with my problems
>   → Finally, as a result of having a partner, I can share my problems easily with him or her and get good advice.

For example cause sentences, look back at your answers to Task B-3-3 on page 67, or search the Internet to find other useful cause and effect sentences.

4. Think about your Concluding Sentence(s)

How will you end your paragraph? Look at several ways below and write your Concluding Sentence(s) in your notebook.

- Summarize your main points using different words.
- Repeat your Topic Sentence using different words.
- Get the reader to think about his/her own relationships with people.

5. Write your draft

Decide roughly how many words you will write and make a note of this in your notebook. Then, start writing a paragraph about your Topic. Remember to include the following information.

- A title
- A Topic Sentence
- Supporting Sentences
- Words/Phrases to show causes and/or effects
- Extra Information Sentences
- Concluding Sentence(s)

E Completing the Draft

1 Practice

In order to complete your draft, you need to read through it and correct any mistakes. Practice checking a draft. Read the paragraph below. Find and correct 15 mistakes. Then, share your answers with your partner.

The effects of having good friends

Most of us are luck to have good friends throughout our lives. Having good friends is beneficial in a number of way. One important effect on our lives is that we are not never lonely. We always have friends to go out with or to chatting with online. We can share many information and news about what we've been doing. we can also get advice about any problems we may have. Another great benefit is that we can learn many things from our friends. For example, they may teach us how to use a new appli on our phone, how to cooking a new dish, or how best to hit a home run in a baseball game. Finally, the most big effect is that friends make our lives fun. Good friends know us listen to us, make us laugh, and support us when they are down. As a result they give important meaning to who and what we are. Therefore, without company of good friends, I'm sure that most peoples' lives would be really less interesting than they are now.

---

2 Check your draft

Check your draft and correct any mistakes you find.

3 Check your partner's draft

Read your partner's draft and check it. If you find any mistakes, tell your partner.

4 Revise your draft

Read your draft again and think of any ways to improve it. Make any necessary revisions.

Unit 9: Summary Paragraphs

Fluency

Topic: Routines

A Getting Started

1 Guess

What are these pictures of? Share your ideas with your partner.

2 Connect

Match a picture to each sentence below. Write **a**–**f** in the boxes.

1. I have a Chinese class on Monday afternoons.
2. I usually get up at 5:30 a.m.
3. I get home at 10:30 p.m.
4. I always go to bed after midnight.
5. I catch the 6:40 train downtown.
6. After school, I work at a convenience store from 6 to 10 p.m.

3 Discuss

Are these sentences true for you?
Share your answers with your partner.

> Sentence #2 is not true for me. I get up at 7:30 a.m.

B Free-writing: Your typical day

1 Think

Get ready to write a paragraph. Think about your typical day.

2 Set the time

Decide how long you will write for and make a note of the time limit in the chart on page 119.

3 Write

Think of the title and Topic Sentence, then write a paragraph in your notebook. Use the examples to help you. Stop writing when the time is up.

> **[Title]**
> A typical day
>
> ....
>
> **[Topic Sentence]**
> There are many things that I usually do on a {day of the week}.

4 Record

How many words did you write? Make a note of the total number in the chart on page 119.

5 Share

Pass your notebook to your partner, then share each other's paragraph. What did you learn about your partner?

> You have no classes on Mondays. That's lucky!

C Practicing Summarizing

1 Understand

When you summarize a paragraph, read it carefully, take notes, and find the writer's Main Ideas. Then, write them using your own words. Do not copy the writer's words. As you can see in the examples below, summaries may only be a few sentences.

[Original paragraph]

I snooze for 15 minutes until my alarm sounds again. After, I get up and take a shower at 5:45 a.m. Then, I get dressed. I have breakfast at 6:10 a.m. I usually eat miso soup and rice. After breakfast, I brush my teeth. I then pack my bag ready for school. I leave my apartment at 6:30 a.m. and head to the train station.

[Possible summaries]

1. It takes him/her 45 minutes to get ready for school.

2. He/She gets ready for school and leaves for the station at 6:30 a.m.

3. He/She gets up at 5:45 a.m., showers, dresses, eats, and leaves for school by 6:30 a.m.

2 Discuss

Answer the questions in pairs/groups.

1. What are the writer's Main Ideas of the original paragraph above?

2. How can you rewrite the following sentences in your own words?

   a. I get up at 5:30 a.m. →

   b. I catch the 6:40 train downtown.

      →

   c. After school, I work at a convenience store from 6 to 10 p.m.

      →

   d. I go to bed at midnight. →

D Summarizing I: Your partner's paragraph

1 Prepare

Read the paragraph your partner wrote in Free-writing, take notes below, and find his/her Main Ideas.

2 Write

Try to shorten the original paragraph. Write a summary below.

How many words are in the original paragraph and your summary?

3 Share

Pass your textbook and return your partner's notebook to him/her, then share each other's summary. How well did your partner summarize your original paragraph?

> It's a good summary, but you missed the part about my dance practice. That's an important part of my typical day.

E Summarizing II: A paragraph on the Internet

1 Prepare

Search the Internet and find an interesting paragraph of someone's typical day. Read it carefully, take notes below, and find the writer's Main Ideas.

2 Write

Try to shorten the original paragraph. Write a summary below.

How many words are in the original paragraph and your summary?

3 Share

Pass your textbook and the original paragraph to your partner, then share each other's summary. How well did your partner summarize the original paragraph?

F Reflecting

Look back

Answer the questions about Unit 9.

1. What did you learn?

2. What did you write about?

3. How many words did you write for the paragraph?
   - Free-writing: _____ words

4. How many words per minute did you write for the paragraph?
   - Free-writing: About _____ words per minute

Unit 10: Summary Paragraphs

Accuracy

Topic: Jobs

A Getting Started

1 Guess

What are these pictures of? Share your ideas with your partner.

2 Connect

Match a picture to each sentence below. Write a–f in the boxes.

1. In the evening, they take it in turns to prepare dinner.
2. After that, the firefighters clean the station.
3. Each firefighter also does one hour of physical training.
4. The first task is to check their equipment is working okay.
5. Throughout the day, the firefighters will respond to emergencies.
6. Firefighters arrive at the station and change into their uniforms.

3 Discuss

What else may firefighters do in a typical day? Share your answers with your partner.

B Analyzing a Typical Day Paragraph

1 Understand

What is a typical day paragraph? Read the information below to find out.

- A typical day paragraph gives the reader information about someone's usual routines.
- The starting sentence is usually the Topic Sentence. It includes the Topic and the Main Idea (what the writer will write about).
- Supporting Sentences are placed after the Topic Sentence and they describe events in someone's typical day in time order.
- The last sentence of the paragraph is the Concluding Sentence. It may show how a typical day ends and bring the paragraph full circle. A writer may use two or more Concluding Sentences at the end of the paragraph.

2 Skim

Quickly read the paragraph below. Find the Topic Sentence, then circle the Topic and underline the Main Idea. Use a different color pen and underline the Concluding Sentence(s).

The job of a firefighter

A typical day for a firefighter begins at 8 a.m. The firefighters arrive at their assigned fire station, change into their uniforms, and start their shift. The firefighters who have worked the night shift can then go home. The first task is to check their equipment is working okay. The fire truck is also checked to make sure it starts and is ready to go. After that, the firefighters wash the truck, clean their equipment, and clean the station. This involves cleaning the living areas and bathrooms. They then have a meeting and decide on the day's activities. Throughout the day, the firefighters will respond to calls about fires, rescues, and medical emergencies. If there are no calls, the firefighters do training to improve their skills. Each firefighter also does one hour of physical training using the gym equipment at the station. In the evening, they take it in turns to prepare dinner. They then eat, clean up the kitchen, and relax. However, they are always ready to respond to emergencies. At around 10 p.m., the firefighters sleep at the station. The shift ends at 8 a.m. the following morning when the new shift of firefighters arrive.

3 Discuss

Read the paragraph again and answer the questions in pairs/groups.

1. What is the Topic of the paragraph?

2. What is the Main Idea of the paragraph?

3. What do firefighters do in a typical day?
   -
   -
   -
   -
   -

4. Find five words/phrases that the writer uses to show time order.

   Ex at 8 a.m.

5. How does the Concluding Sentence(s) link to the Topic Sentence?

C Practicing Summarizing

1 Prepare

Before writing a Summary Paragraph, you need to take short notes of the writer's Main Ideas in the original paragraph. Your notes should include the most important information only. Read the paragraph on page 80 again, then look at the example notes below.

The job of a firefighter
8 a.m. – begin shift
1st task – check equipment, then clean
Next – meeting
At any time – respond to emergencies
Also – training
Evening – dinner
10 p.m. – sleep
8 a.m. next day – end shift

2 Write

When writing a Summary Paragraph, at first you should look at your notes only. Finally, check your summary with the original paragraph. Remember the points below.

- Your summary should be much shorter than the original paragraph.
- It should contain only information in the original paragraph.
- Use your own words: Do not copy from the original paragraph.
- Include a citation (name of writer, year of publication) at the end.

3 Analyze

The original paragraph on page 80 has 197 words. Read the three summaries below and decide which is the best one. Share your answer with your partner and explain the reasons.

[Summary 1 (59 words)]

    A typical day for a firefighter begins at 8 a.m. Throughout the day, the firefighters will respond to calls about emergencies. Otherwise, they check their equipment is working fine and clean the truck and station. At the station, they do training to improve their skills and do physical training to stay fit. Their shift ends at 8 a.m. the following morning (Boon, 2017).

[Summary 2 (49 words)]

    Firefighters usually start work at 8 a.m. They are on call all day to deal with emergencies. Otherwise, they spend their day by making sure their equipment is working fine and the station is clean. They also do exercises and practice firefighting. They finish work at 8 a.m. the next day (Boon, 2017).

[Summary 3 (50 words)]

    Firefighters have a dangerous job. They start work at 8 a.m. most days. They wait for emergency calls and put out fires. At the station, they make sure their equipment works and everything is clean. They also do training. Some firefighters practice karate. They finish work at 8 a.m. the next morning (Boon, 2017).

D Summarizing a Paragraph

1 Prepare

Choose one of the example paragraphs below as the original paragraph. Then, take short notes of the writer's Main Ideas in your notebook.

- The talent competition (Unit 2: pages 18-19)
- My favorite place (Unit 4: page 32)
- High school and university life (Unit 6: pages 46-47)
- How good friendship happens (Unit 8: pages 66-67)

2 Write

Look at your notes and write a summary in your notebook. Then, check your summary with the points below.

1. Is it much shorter than the original paragraph?
2. Does it contain information only in the original paragraph?
3. Are the sentences rewritten with your own words?
4. Does it include a citation (name of writer, year of publication) at the end?

3 Check your partner's summary

Find a classmate who chose the same example paragraph as you did. Read your partner's summary and check it. If you find any mistakes, tell your partner.

4 Revise your summary

Read your summary again and think of any ways to improve it. Make any necessary revisions.

5 Vote on the best summary

Make a group of classmates who chose the same example paragraph, then read their summaries. Vote on the best summary in your group.

E Writing and Summarizing a Paragraph

1 Think

Get ready to write a typical day paragraph of a popular job. Search the Internet and get information.

2 Write your draft

Start writing a paragraph. Remember to include the information below.

- A title
- A Topic Sentence
- Supporting Sentences
- Words/Phrases to show time order
- Concluding Sentence(s)

3 Check your draft

Check your draft and correct any mistakes you find.

4 Check your partner's draft

Read your partner's draft and check it. If you find any mistakes, tell your partner.

5 Revise your draft

Read your draft again and think of any ways to improve it. Make any necessary revisions.

6 Prepare

Get ready to summarize a typical day paragraph of a popular job. Pass your notebook to your partner, then read your partner's draft. Take notes below and find his/her Main Ideas.

7 Summarize

Try to shorten the original paragraph. Write a summary below.

How many words are in the original paragraph and your summary?

8 Share

Pass your partner's notebook and your textbook to your partner, then share each other's summary. How well did your partner summarize your original paragraph?

Unit 11 Opinion Paragraphs

Topic Issues

Fluency

A Getting Started

1 Guess

What are these pictures of? Share your ideas with your partner.

2 Connect

Match a picture to each opinion below. Write **a**–**f** in the boxes.

1. It is better to work in a group than to work individually.
2. Young people should not give up their seats on the trains.
3. Cheating on a test is a bad idea for several reasons.
4. In my opinion, the drinking age in Japan should not be lowered.
5. It can be argued that breakfast is the most important meal of the day.
6. It is important to start job-hunting early at university.

3 Discuss

Do you agree with these opinions?
Share your answers with your partner.

> I'm against opinion #6. I want to concentrate on studying before doing job-hunting.

B Free-writing I: Your opinion

1 Think

Get ready to write an Opinion Paragraph. Choose one of the opinions from Task A-2 on page 87. If you are for the opinion, use it as your Topic Sentence. If you are against it, change the Topic Sentence to reflect your different opinion.

2 Set the time

Decide how long you will write for and make a note of the time limit in the chart on page 119.

3 Write

Think of a title, then write a paragraph including the Topic Sentence in your notebook. Use the example to help you. Stop writing when the time is up.

> **[Title]**
> Working in a group
>
> **[Topic Sentence]**
> I believe it is better to work individually than to work in a group.

4 Record

How many words did you write? Make a note of the total number in the chart on page 119.

5 Share

Pass your notebook to your partner, then share each other's paragraph. What did you learn about your partner's opinion?

> You don't think breakfast is important because you don't have time to eat it in the morning. Right?

C Researching

1 Think

In order to write an Opinion Paragraph, it is useful to know how people usually express their opinions in sentences, and how they add points and give examples. Look at the example search term below to get such information.

- opinion paragraphs useful language
-
-
-

What other search terms may help you? Add them to the list, then share your ideas with your partner.

2 Get information

Search the Internet. Use the example notes below to help you. Write down what you find in your notebook. Then, share the information with your classmates.

[Opinion Paragraphs]

– Useful language

  http://www.eoioviedo.org/trabajos/EOIwriting_bank/OPINION.pdf

  - I believe…
  - In my opinion,

– Example paragraphs

  https://e-writing.wikispaces.com/Opinion+Paragraph

D Free-writing II: Your opinion

1 Think

Get ready to write an Opinion Paragraph. Choose one opinion from Task A-2 on page 87 that is different from your choice for Free-writing I. If you are for the opinion, use it as your Topic Sentence. If you are against it, change the Topic Sentence to reflect your different opinion. Use information you found on the Internet to help you with your paragraph.

2 Set the time

Decide how long you will write for and make a note of the time limit in the chart on page 119.

3 Write

Think of a title, then write a paragraph including the Topic Sentence in your notebook. Stop writing when the time is up.

4 Record

How many words did you write? Make a note of the total number in the chart on page 119.

5 Share

Pass your notebook to your partner, then share each other's paragraph. What did you learn about your partner's opinion?

> You don't want to give up your seat on the train because you've waited in line a long time for it. You want to sleep, right?

E Free-writing III: Your classmates' opinions

1 Think

Get ready to write an Opinion Paragraph. Think of your own Topics and write opinion sentences in your notebook. Then, decide which opinion you will use as the Topic Sentence.

2 Interview

Tell your opinion to your classmates and ask them the following questions. Take notes as you listen to the answers.

- Do you agree or disagree?
- Why?
- What other reasons do you have?

3 Set the time

Decide how long you will write for and make a note of the time limit in the chart on page 119.

4 Write

Write a paragraph in your notebook. Stop writing when the time is up.

5 Record

How many words did you write? Make a note of the total number in the chart on page 119.

6 Share

Pass your notebook to your partner, then share each other's paragraph. What did you find out about your partner's and classmates' opinions?

F Reflecting

▶ Look back

Answer the questions about Unit 11.

1. What did you learn?

2. What did you write about?

3. How many words did you write for each paragraph?
   - Free-writing I: _____ words
   - Free-writing II: _____ words
   - Free-writing III: _____ words

4. How many words per minute did you write for each paragraph?
   - Free-writing I: About _____ words per minute
   - Free-writing II: About _____ words per minute
   - Free-writing III: About _____ words per minute

Unit 12 Opinion Paragraphs

Topic Smartphones

Accuracy

A Getting Started

1 Guess

What are these pictures of? Share your ideas with your partner.

2 Connect

Match a picture to each sentence below. Write a–f in the boxes.

1. This can be very annoying and make other people really angry.
2. People should keep smartphones in their pockets or bags while walking.
3. Two business people began to fight after bumping into each other.
4. Finally, using a smartphone while walking could be deadly.
5. People looking down at smartphones do not see their friends.
6. It is also easy to walk past beautiful rivers and amazing wildlife.

3 Discuss

What is the writer's opinion? How may the writer support his/her argument? Share your answers with your partner.

B Analyzing an Opinion Paragraph

1 Understand

What is an Opinion Paragraph? Read the information below to find out.

- An Opinion Paragraph discusses the writer's view on a Topic. The writer tells the reader whether he/she is for or against the opinion and gives reasons to support his/her argument.
- The starting sentence is usually the Topic Sentence. It includes the Topic and the Main Idea (whether the writer is for or against the opinion).
- Supporting Sentences are placed after the Topic Sentence and they give reasons to support the writer's argument.
- Extra Information Sentences give more information about each main point.
- In order to support his/her argument, a writer may include summaries and citations (writer's name and year of publication) of other writers' works.
- The last sentence of the paragraph is the Concluding Sentence. It reminds the reader of the Topic and summarizes the main arguments in the paragraph. A writer may use two or more Concluding Sentences at the end of the paragraph.
- If a writer includes citations, a reference list is needed at the end of the paragraph.

2 Skim

Quickly read the paragraph below. Find the Topic Sentence, then circle the Topic and underline the Main Idea. Use a different color pen and underline the Concluding Sentence(s).

Do not be a smartphone zombie

Have you ever had to jump out of the way of people on the streets while they were using their smartphones? In my opinion, people should not use their smartphones while walking. Firstly, it is very easy for them to walk into other people when they are looking down at a screen. This can be very annoying and make other people really angry. I have seen a number of cases at train stations where people have started to shout and push each other. I have also seen two business people begin to fight after one person bumped into the other. Another reason not to use a smartphone while walking is that it is easy to miss something important. For example, imagine a good friend walks by and says, "Hello!" A person looking down at his/her smartphone would not see the friend or reply to the greeting. The friend would then feel sad. It is also easy to walk past famous buildings, green trees, beautiful rivers, and amazing wildlife without seeing anything. Finally, using a smartphone while walking could be deadly. There are stories of people being hit by trains or falling into seas and dying or nearly dying (Sharp, 2015). These deadly or near-deadly accidents were caused by people not paying attention to their surroundings. Taking everything into consideration, to remain safe and to see more, people should keep their smartphones in their pockets or bags while walking down the street.

Reference:
Sharp, M. (2015, March 02). Beware the smartphone zombies blindly wandering around Hong Kong. *South China Morning Post*. Retrieved from: http://www.scmp.com/lifestyle/technology/article/1725001/smartphone-zombies-are-putting-your-life-and-theirs-danger

3 Discuss

Read the paragraph again and answer the questions in pairs/groups.

1. What is the Topic of the paragraph?

2. What is the Main Idea of the paragraph?

3. What three reasons does the writer include in the paragraph to support his/her argument?
   -
   -
   -

4. What extra information does the writer provide about each reason?
   -
   -
   -

5. The writer includes a short summary of another writer's work on smartphone zombies. Answer the questions below.

   a. What is the name of the writer?

   b. What is the year of publication?

   c. What kind of publication is it?

   d. Why did the writer include the summary?

6. How does the Concluding Sentence(s) link to the Topic Sentence?

Unit 12 Opinion Paragraphs Accuracy

C Mind-mapping

1 Understand

Look at the mind-map below. This shows the writer's ideas before writing the paragraph you read on page 95.

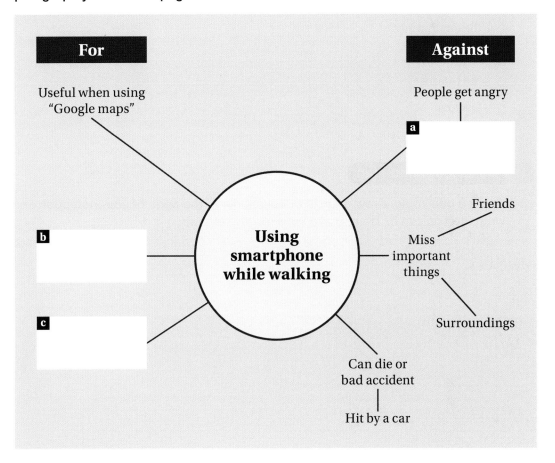

2 Discuss

Look at the mind-map again and answer the questions in pairs/groups.

1. Read the paragraph on page 95 again and complete box **a** in the mind-map with the missing information.
2. Complete boxes **b** and **c** in the mind-map with two reasons for using smartphones while walking.

97

3 Prepare

Think of possible Topics for an Opinion Paragraph. Then, write them in your notebook, referring to the examples below.

- studying English
- smoking
- the environment
- the Olympics
- the Internet
- fast food

4 Make your mind-map

Choose one Topic. Draw a circle in the middle of the page of your notebook and write the Topic in it. Then, make your own mind-map.

D Draft-writing: Your opinion

1 Prepare

Search the Internet and find other writers' works about your Topic. Read them carefully and take notes about the points below.

- Each writer's arguments for or against
- Interesting examples used to support the arguments
- Each writer's name
- The year of publication of the book or article

Choose one or two arguments and/or examples, then summarize them in your notebook.

2 Plan your paragraph

Look at your mind-map and the notes you made in Task D-1, then decide whether you are for or against your Topic. Think of the title of your paragraph and make a plan of how best to order your main points, referring to the example below. Also, think about where in your paragraph you can use other writers' opinions to support your argument.

> Do not be a smartphone zombie
> 1. Topic Sentence – should not use their smartphones while walking
> 2. Easy to walk into people
> 3. Can miss things
> 4. Can be deadly – use summary of (Sharp, 2015) here
> 5. Concluding Sentence(s) – keep smartphones in pocket or bag

Remember that your plan will be important when you think about your Supporting Sentences later.

3 Decide on your Topic Sentence

Think about your Topic and Main Idea, then plan your Topic Sentence. Write four different Topic Sentences in your notebook, referring to the examples below.

> 1. In my opinion, people should not use their smartphones while walking.
> 2. There are many reasons why using a smartphone while walking is a bad idea.
> 3. I think people should think twice before using their smartphones while walking.
> 4. Using a smartphone while walking is not a sensible thing to do for several reasons.

Show your four Topic Sentences to your partner and ask his/her opinion. Then, decide which one you like the best.

4 Think about your Supporting Sentences

Look at the plan you made in Task D-2. Then, write your Supporting Sentences in your notebook for each main reason you will give the reader to support your argument. For example sentences, look back at your answers to Task B-3-3 on page 96.

5 Think about your Concluding Sentence(s)

How will you end your paragraph? Look at several ways below and write your Concluding Sentence(s) in your notebook.

> - Summarize your main arguments using different words.
> - Repeat your Topic Sentence using different words.
> - Make a suggestion to the reader.

6 Write your draft

Decide roughly how many words you will write and make a note of this in your notebook. Then, start writing a paragraph about your Topic. Remember to include the following information.

- A title
- A Topic Sentence
- Supporting Sentences
- Extra Information Sentences
- At least one summary and citation
- Concluding Sentence(s)
- A reference list

E Completing the Draft

1 Practice

In order to complete your draft, you need to read through it and correct any mistakes. Practice checking a draft. Read the paragraph below. Find and correct 15 mistakes. Then, share your answers with your partner.

Smartphone users are not zombies

Recently, people have been criticized for using our smartphones while walking. I don't think this is fair for several reasons. First of all, people needs to use their smartphones when outside. For example applications like "Google maps" are very useful to find places. Often, when I use "Google maps," I am careful to look ahead while walking. I stop to walk when I look at the screen. Moreover, these days, most people need to check their massages at all times. For example, when meeting friends. People can quickly check their screens to see if they have any new notification. Final point is that smartphones have become an essential part of most people lives. As a result, people are change too (Robertson, 2016). They're learning to walk and use their phone while also pay attention to their surroundings. In this way, they are not "smartphone zombies," but talented multitaskers.

Reference:

Lobertson, D. (February 22). *Smartphone zombies are taking over our pavements. Am I the only one who thinks that's a good thing?* Retrieved from: http://www.independent.co.uk/voices/smartphone-zombies-are-taking-over-our-pavements-am-i-the-only-person-who-thinks-thats-a-good-thing-a6887551.html

2 **Check your draft**

Check your draft and correct any mistakes you find.

3 **Check your partner's draft**

Read your partner's draft and check it. If you find any mistakes, tell your partner.

4 **Revise your draft**

Read your draft again and think of any ways to improve it. Make any necessary revisions.

Review 2

Review Tasks for Units 7–12

Unit 7 Cause and Effect Paragraphs — Accuracy

1 Look back

You practiced writing for fluency in Unit 7. What did you study? What did you write about? Share your answers with your partner.

2 Review common mistakes

Look at your answers for Task E-1 in Unit 2 (page 24), Unit 4 (page 38), Unit 6 (page 51), Unit 8 (page 72), and Unit 12 (page 101) to review the common mistakes made when writing.

3 Check your drafts

Now, you will focus on accuracy using your drafts for Free-writing I, II, and III. Check your drafts in your notebook and correct any mistakes you find.

4 Check your partner's drafts

Read your partner's drafts and check them. If you find any mistakes, tell your partner.

5 Revise for accuracy

Read your drafts again and think of any ways to improve them. Make any necessary revisions.

Unit 8 Cause and Effect Paragraphs

Fluency

1 Look back

You practiced writing for accuracy in Unit 8. What did you study? What did you write about? Share your answers with your partner.

2 Think

In Unit 8, you wrote a Cause and/or Effect Paragraph about relationships between people. Now, get ready to write a new Cause and/or Effect Paragraph. Think about another Topic to write about. Refer to the examples in Task C-3 on page 69 to help you.

3 Set the time

Now, you will practice writing for fluency. Decide how long you will write for and make a note of the time limit in the chart on page 119.

4 Write for fluency

Write a paragraph in your notebook. Stop writing when the time is up.

5 Record

How many words did you write? Make a note of the total number in the chart on page 119.

6 Share

Pass your notebook to your partner, then share each other's paragraph. What did you learn about your partner's ideas?

Unit 9 Summary Paragraphs

Accuracy

1 Look back

You practiced writing for fluency and summarizing paragraphs in Unit 9. What did you study? What did you write about and summarize? Share your answers with your partner.

2 Review common mistakes

Look at your answers for Task E-1 in Unit 2 (page 24), Unit 4 (page 38), Unit 6 (page 51), Unit 8 (page 72), and Unit 12 (page 101) to review the common mistakes made when writing.

3 Check your drafts

Now, you will focus on accuracy using your draft for Free-writing. Check your draft in your notebook and correct any mistakes you find.

4 Check your partner's drafts

Read your partner's draft and check it. If you find any mistakes, tell your partner.

5 Revise for accuracy

Read your draft again and think of any ways to improve it. Make any necessary revisions.

Review 2
Review Tasks for Units 7–12

6 Prepare

Pass your notebook to your partner, then read your partner's draft. Take notes below and find his/her Main Ideas.

7 Summarize

Try to shorten the original paragraph. Write a summary below.

How many words are in the original paragraph and your summary?

8 Share

Pass your partner's notebook and your textbook to your partner, then share each other's summary. How well did your partner summarize your original paragraph?

Unit 10 Summary Paragraphs   Fluency

1 Look back

You practiced writing for accuracy and summarizing paragraphs in Unit 10. What did you study? What did you write about and summarize? Share your answers with your partner.

2 Think

In Unit 10, you wrote a typical day paragraph of a popular job. Now, get ready to write a new typical day paragraph. Search the Internet and get information of another popular job.

3 Set the time

Now, you will practice writing for fluency. Decide how long you will write for and make a note of the time limit in the chart on page 119.

4 Write for fluency

Write a paragraph in your notebook. Stop writing when the time is up.

5 Record

How many words did you write? Make a note of the total number in the chart on page 119.

Review 2

Review Tasks for Units 7–12

6 Prepare

Pass your notebook to your partner, then read your partner's draft. Take notes below and find his/her Main Ideas.

7 Summarize

Try to shorten the original paragraph. Write a summary below.

How many words are in the original paragraph and your summary?

8 Share

Pass your partner's notebook and your textbook to your partner, then share each other's summary. How well did your partner summarize your original paragraph?

Unit 11 Opinion Paragraphs — Accuracy

1 Look back

You practiced writing for fluency in Unit 11. What did you study? What did you write about? Share your answers with your partner.

2 Review common mistakes

Look at your answers for Task E-1 in Unit 2 (page 24), Unit 4 (page 38), Unit 6 (page 51), Unit 8 (page 72), and Unit 12 (page 101) to review the common mistakes made when writing.

3 Check your drafts

Now, you will focus on accuracy using your drafts for Free-writing I, II, and III. Check your drafts in your notebook and correct any mistakes you find.

4 Check your partner's drafts

Read your partner's drafts and check them. If you find any mistakes, tell your partner.

5 Revise for accuracy

Read your drafts again and think of any ways to improve them. Make any necessary revisions.

Review 2
Review Tasks for Units 7–12

Unit 12 Opinion Paragraphs — Fluency

1 Look back

You practiced writing for accuracy in Unit 12. What did you study? What did you write about? Share your answers with your partner.

2 Think

In Unit 12, you wrote an Opinion Paragraph about a chosen Topic. Now, get ready to write a new Opinion Paragraph. Think about another Topic to write about. Refer to the examples in Task C-3 on page 98 to help you.

3 Set the time

Now, you will practice writing for fluency. Decide how long you will write for and make a note of the time limit in the chart on page 119.

4 Write for fluency

Write a paragraph in your notebook. Stop writing when the time is up.

5 Record

How many words did you write? Make a note of the total number in the chart on page 119.

6 Share

Pass your notebook to your partner, then share each other's paragraph. What did you learn about your partner's opinion?

Assignment 1

Narrative Paragraphs

1 Search the Internet and find five Topics for Narrative Paragraphs.

> **Ex** My first day at school
> -
> -
> -
> -
> -

2 Choose one Topic and make a mind-map as you did on page 21.

3 Look at your mind-map and choose what you would like to write about. Then, think of the title of your paragraph and make a list of the events in time order.

4 Think about your Topic and Main Idea, then decide on your Topic Sentence.

5 Look at the list you have made. Then, think about your Supporting Sentences with time phrases as you did on page 23.

6 Think about your Concluding Sentence(s), referring to the different ways to end a paragraph on page 23.

7 Decide roughly how many words you will write and make a note of this. Then, start writing a paragraph. Remember to include the information below.

> - A title
> - A Topic Sentence
> - Supporting Sentences (with time phrases)
> - Concluding Sentence(s)

8 Check your draft and correct any mistakes you find.

9 In order to complete your draft, read it again and think of any ways to improve it. Make any necessary revisions.

Assignment 2 — Descriptive Paragraphs

1 Search the Internet and find five Topics for Descriptive Paragraphs.

> **Ex** Describe a room in your home
> •
> •
> •
> •
> •

2 Choose one Topic and make a mind-map as you did on page 35.

3 Look at your mind-map and choose what you would like to write about. Then, think of the title of your paragraph and make a plan of how best to describe your chosen Topic.

4 Think about your Topic and Main Idea, then decide on your Topic Sentence.

5 Look at the plan you have made. Then, think about your Supporting Sentences and Extra Information Sentences as you did on pages 36–37.

6 Think about your Concluding Sentence(s), referring to the different ways to end a paragraph on page 37.

7 Decide roughly how many words you will write and make a note of this. Then, start writing a paragraph. Remember to include the information below.

> • A title
> • A Topic Sentence
> • Supporting Sentences
> • Extra Information Sentences
> • Concluding Sentence(s)

8 Check your draft and correct any mistakes you find.

9 In order to complete your draft, read it again and think of any ways to improve it. Make any necessary revisions.

Assignment 3
Compare and Contrast Paragraphs

1 Search the Internet and find five Topics (Subjects A and B) for Compare and Contrast Paragraphs.

> **Ex** Two cities (Tokyo and Osaka)
> -
> -
> -
> -
> -

2 Choose one Topic (Subjects A and B) and make a list as you did on page 48.

3 Look at your list and decide whether you will compare and/or contrast the Topic (Subjects A and B). Then, think of the title of your paragraph and make a plan of how best to order your main points.

4 Think about your Topic (Subjects A and B) and Main Idea, then decide on your Topic Sentence.

5 Look at the plan you have made. Then, think about your Supporting Sentences with words/phrases to show comparison and/or contrast as you did on page 50.

6 Think about your Concluding Sentence(s), referring to the different ways to end a paragraph on page 50.

7 Decide roughly how many words you will write and make a note of this. Then, start writing a paragraph. Remember to include the information below.

> - A title
> - A Topic Sentence
> - Supporting Sentences
> - Words/Phrases to show comparison and/or contrast
> - Extra Information Sentences
> - Concluding Sentence(s)

8 Check your draft and correct any mistakes you find.

9 In order to complete your draft, read it again and think of any ways to improve it. Make any necessary revisions.

Assignment 4

Cause and Effect Paragraphs

1 Search the Internet and find five Topics for Cause and Effect Paragraphs.

> **Ex** Smartphone use
>
> -
> -
> -
> -
> -

2 Choose one Topic and make a list as you did on page 69.

3 Look at your list and decide decide whether you will write about the causes and/or effects of your Topic. Then, think of the title of your paragraph and make a plan of how best to order your main points.

4 Think about your Topic and Main Idea, then decide on your Topic Sentence.

5 Look at the plan you have made. Then, think about your Supporting Sentences with words/phrases to show causes and/or effects as you did on page 71.

6 Think about your Concluding Sentence(s), referring to the different ways to end a paragraph on page 71.

7 Decide roughly how many words you will write and make a note of this. Then, start writing a paragraph. Remember to include the information below.

> - A title
> - A Topic Sentence
> - Supporting Sentences
> - Words/Phrases to show causes and/or effects
> - Extra Information Sentences
> - Concluding Sentence(s)

8 Check your draft and correct any mistakes you find.

9 In order to complete your draft, read it again and think of any ways to improve it. Make any necessary revisions.

Assignment 5

Summary Paragraphs

1 Search the Internet and research a typical day paragraph. Find a different job to the one you chose in Task E-1 for Unit 10 on page 85.

2 Start writing a paragraph. Remember to include the information below.

- A title
- A Topic Sentence
- Supporting Sentences
- Words/Phrases to show time order
- Concluding Sentence(s)

3 Check your draft and correct any mistakes you find.

4 In order to complete your draft, read it again and think of any ways to improve it. Make any necessary revisions.

5 Send your draft to a classmate.

6 Read your classmate's draft. Take notes and find his/her Main ideas.

7 Try to shorten your classmate's original paragraph. Write a summary.

8 How many words are in your classmate's original paragraph and your summary?

Assignment 6: Opinion Paragraphs

1 Search the Internet and find five Topics for Opinion Paragraphs.

> **Ex** Do sports stars get paid too much money?

-
-
-
-
-

2 Choose one Topic and make a mind-map as you did on page 98.

3 Search the Internet and find other writers' works about your Topic. Read them carefully and take notes about the points below.

- Each writer's arguments for or against
- Interesting examples used to support the arguments
- Each writer's name
- The year of publication of the book or article

Choose one or two arguments and/or examples, then summarize them in your notebook.

4 Look at your mind-map and the notes you have made, then decide whether you are for or against your Topic. Think of the title of your paragraph and make a plan of how best to order your main points. Also, think about where in your paragraph you can use other writers' opinions to support your argument.

5 Think about your Topic and Main Idea, then decide on your Topic Sentence.

6 Look at the plan you have made. Then, think about your Supporting Sentences for each main reason you will give the reader to support your argument as you did on page 100.

7 Think about your Concluding Sentence(s), referring to the different ways to end a paragraph on page 100.

8 Decide roughly how many words you will write and make a note of this. Then, start writing a paragraph. Remember to include the information below.

- A title
- Supporting Sentences
- Extra Information Sentences
- At least one summary and citation
- Concluding Sentence(s)
- A reference list

9 Check your draft and correct any mistakes you find.

10 In order to complete your draft, read it again and think of any ways to improve it. Make any necessary revisions.

Chart for Recording

		Time (min.)	Words	Date
Unit 1	Free-writing I			
	Free-writing II			
	Free-writing III			
Unit 3	Free-writing I			
	Free-writing II			
	Free-writing III			
Unit 5	Free-writing I			
	Free-writing II			
	Free-writing III			
Review 1	Unit 2			
	Unit 4			
	Unit 6			
Unit 7	Free-writing I			
	Free-writing II			
	Free-writing III			
Unit 9	Free-writing			
Unit 11	Free-writing I			
	Free-writing II			
	Free-writing III			
Review 2	Unit 8			
	Unit 10			
	Unit 12			

Writing for Fluency and Accuracy
2つのアプローチで学ぶパラグラフ・ライティング

2017年1月20日　初版発行
2023年3月30日　第 4 刷

著　者	Andy Boon
発行者	松村達生
発行所	センゲージ ラーニング株式会社

〒102-0073　東京都千代田区九段北1-11-11　第2フナトビル5階
電話 03-3511-4392　FAX 03-3511-4391
e-mail: eltjapan@cengage.com
copyright©2017 センゲージ ラーニング株式会社

装　丁	足立友幸 (parastyle)
編集協力	飯尾緑子 (parastyle)
イラスト	大塚砂織
印刷・製本	株式会社平河工業社

ISBN 978-4-86312-306-9

もし落丁、乱丁、その他不良品がありましたら、お取り替えいたします。本書の全部、または一部を無断で複写(コピー)することは、著作権法上での例外を除き、禁じられていますのでご注意ください。